WHAT'S THE BIG DEAL ABOUT

Americans

WHAT'S THE BIG DEAL ABOUT
Americans

written by **Ruby Shamir**
illustrated by **Matt Faulkner**

PHILOMEL BOOKS

PHILOMEL BOOKS
An imprint of Penguin Random House LLC, New York

First published in picture book format by Philomel Books,
an imprint of Penguin Random House LLC, 2019.
Chapter book first published in the United States of America
by Philomel Books, an imprint of Penguin Random House LLC, 2020.

Visit us online at penguinrandomhouse.com

THE LIBRARY OF CONGRESS HAS CATALOGED THE PICTURE BOOK EDITION AS FOLLOWS:
Library of Congress Cataloging-in-Publication Data
Names: Shamir, Ruby, author. | Faulkner, Matt, illustrator.
Title: What's the big deal about Americans? / Ruby Shamir ; illustrated by Matt Faulkner. |
Description: New York, NY : Philomel Books, [2019] | Audience: Age 4–8. |
Audience: Grade K to 3. | Identifiers: LCCN 2018021026 | ISBN 9781524738037
(hardcover) | ISBN 9781524738068 (e-book) | Subjects: LCSH: United States—
Civilization—Juvenile literature. | Popular culture—United States—Juvenile literature. |
Americans—Juvenile literature. |
Classification: LCC E169.12 .S46 2019 | DDC 973—dc23
LC record available at https://lccn.loc.gov/2018021026

HC ISBN 9780593116395
PB ISBN 9780593116364

Manufactured in China by
RR Donnelley Asia Printing Solutions Ltd.
1 3 5 7 9 10 8 6 4 2

Chapter book edited by Talia Benamy. Original picture book edited by Jill Santopolo.
Design by Jennifer Chung. Text set in Adobe Jenson Pro.

The art was created in three stages: first, thumbnail sketches—many small sketches
created for each illustration emphasizing page design, visual narrative, and light source; second,
intermediate sketches—several sketches created to refine the design of the book's characters
and their environment, details, etc.; and third, the final art, which was created with
watercolor and pencil on sanded Arches 140 lb. cold press paper.

To my parents, Ami and Nira Shamir,

who came from across the sea to make America our home.

—R.S.

Dedicated to my dear sister, Stacey.

And to Kris, always.

—M.F.

WHAT'S AMERICA MADE OF?

Have you ever baked cookies? It may seem strange to add salt to the dough when a cookie is supposed to be sweet, but without it, the cookies just wouldn't taste right. A surprising mix of ingredients makes the tastiest treats.

Now here's a silly idea: imagine America as a giant cookie. What's in our cookie dough? Why, we are, of course! You, your friends, your family, and millions of folks you haven't met. All kinds of people come here from all over the world to live together, share ideas, and create new traditions out of a jumble of old memories and customs.

The ice cream cone is one example of a treat created in the great mixing bowl that is America. When an ice cream booth at a big fair in St. Louis in 1904 ran out of bowls, food sellers from Syria, Lebanon, Turkey, and Ohio in neighboring stalls created waffle cones, edible dishes that allowed visitors to eat their ice cream on the go.

As President Lyndon Johnson said in 1965 when he signed a law welcoming people to America from all over the world, "Our beautiful America was built by a nation of strangers ... nourished by so many cultures and traditions and peoples." That's one smart cookie!

What are the unexpected ingredients that come together in America? How would you describe the rainbow assortment of people who live here? What's the big deal about Americans anyway?

What's more American than apple pie? Like many Americans, the apple pie has roots all over the world. The pie arrived here from England and met German pastries, which lent it a flaky crust. Even the sweet apples in its filling were originally from the area that we know today as Kazakhstan!

WHERE DID AMERICANS COME FROM?

Whether our ancestors traveled here centuries ago or we arrived here yesterday, Americans have come from all over the world, and at some point all of us were new to this land.

The first people here were hundreds of Native American tribes long before the America we know today was formed.

Different tribes had different traditions, languages, and beliefs. Some lived near the oceans and fished for food, while others roamed the plains and hunted buffalo. Some farmed lush river valleys where they spent their whole lives, and others moved from place to place with the changing seasons. Some built cities with homes and temples on huge mounds of earth as tall as a ten-story building, and one built a village on a rock so high that it's called Sky City.

Then, about 500 years ago, explorers came to American shores on boats that had crossed the Atlantic Ocean from Europe. Many stayed and

made a home for themselves in this new land. They brought a lot of changes with them, including animals like horses and cattle, and crops like wheat and rice. In time, they set up our government and way of life. But, as more and more people came to America, the lives of the Native Americans changed forever—and not for the better.

Christopher Columbus was the first European explorer to make land in the Americas during the Age of Exploration. His voyage showed Europeans two whole continents filled with people, ways of life, wildlife, and precious metals that were new to them and very valuable. Tragically, Columbus and many Europeans after him hurt and enslaved the Native American people they met.

The European settlers who came to America built their new homes in areas called colonies, and the settlers were known as colonists. The first successful English colony in America was in Jamestown, Virginia, where about 100 colonists arrived in 1607. Members of the Algonquin nation began trading with them and taught them how to grow crops. The chief's daughter, Pocahontas, even married an English settler. But as Jamestown grew and thrived, settlers there and in other colonies pushed Native Americans off their lands.

WHY DO PEOPLE COME HERE?

Has your family ever moved? Maybe you moved to a bigger house when your family grew. Or maybe you moved to a new town because your mom got a new job. Maybe you moved to America as a refugee, seeking safety from danger and war in your home country.

Migration is when people move to new places. Immigration is when they move to another country, where they are immigrants.

Throughout our history, immigrants have flocked to America by land, sea, and air. When immigrants arrived at Ellis Island in New York City, they saw the poem on the base of the nearby Statue of Liberty, which says, "Give me your tired, your poor, Your huddled masses yearning to breathe free . . ." Whether they arrived on foot, or by boat, train, car, or airplane, most people moved here to make their lives better and their kids' futures brighter.

A lot of immigrants have been refugees, including the brilliant scientist Albert Einstein, basketball star Luol Deng, and writer Isabel Allende. When our first female secretary of state, Madeleine Albright, escaped her home country of Czechoslovakia as a kid, she wasn't sure if she'd ever fit in in America. "I should not have worried," she later realized, "America's embrace is as broad as the country itself."

Every year, more people want to come to America than our rules allow. How should we decide who gets to come? What should America do about families from other countries who need a safe place to live, people who want to enjoy the freedoms we have here in America?

HOW ELSE DID PEOPLE COME TO AMERICA?

Sadly, for several centuries after Europeans settled here, slave traders kidnapped millions of Africans from their villages, separated them from their families, and brought them across the sea against their will as slaves. They and their descendants—their children and grandchildren and great-grandchildren—wouldn't be free until slavery was finally ended in America many generations later.

Enslaved people suffered and were denied every possible freedom, but they stood up for the right to learn, to protect their families, and, ultimately, to be free. Crispus Attucks, whose dad was an African slave and whose mom was a Native American, was one of the early heroes of the American Revolution. He stood up for freedom by standing up to British soldiers in one of the first fights that triggered America's War of Independence.

The brilliant poet Phillis Wheatley was around thirteen years old when she had her first poem published in a newspaper. Even though she was kept as a slave, she learned to read and write, and nothing could hide the light of her poetry.

George Washington Carver was born to an enslaved mother. Through hard work and effort, he eventually became a scientist and professor. He taught farmers creative ways to improve their soil and grow more crops. He became famous as the "Peanut Man" for encouraging Southern farmers, especially African Americans who lived in poverty, to grow the healthy plant.

From protest to poetry to peanuts and beyond, all Americans should be free to follow their dreams.

WHAT DO
AMERICANS EAT?

Peanuts and peanut butter became a big deal in America, feeding everyone from families at home to soldiers fighting in wars far away. But visitors to America don't expect to eat any one specific American dish. Why? Because there's no such thing, even though there are foods that were first grown or invented here.

Ever wonder where your movie popcorn came from? The corn plant is native to the Americas and was cherished by many Native American cultures. The Pawnees grew ten types of corn, and considered one holy. Hidatsa women and girls who tended their corn would sing to it. Corn, squash, and beans are called the "three sisters," and together make a healthy dish we still call by its Algonquin name, succotash.

But many of the foods Americans love most

arrived here with immigrants. Hot dogs and pretzels were originally from Germany, pizza came from Italy, and nachos were first made in Mexico.

Are there special foods that your family loves? Try asking some adults in your life where their favorite recipes came from!

Next time you chow down on a bowl of cereal before rushing out in the morning, you can thank American brothers Will and John Kellogg for inventing the breakfast cereal flake. They made the first flakes out of a bowl of mush accidentally left out overnight!

WHAT LANGUAGE DO AMERICANS SPEAK?

Americans speak lots of languages! English is the language of most storefronts, highway signs, and schools, and it's hard to get very far without knowing it. But there isn't any rule in America that you have to speak English.

In cities and towns where people from different countries meet, words from different languages get jumbled up. Over time, this has changed American English, often making it more interesting and exciting. For example, Louisiana has a rich mix of African, Caribbean, Native American,

How do you say good-bye? "Ciao," "adios," "sayonara," and "au revoir" are all ways of saying "so long" in other languages that have become, well, at least as American as apple pie!

and European cultures. Gumbo, the word for a delicious Louisiana stew, comes from the word "nkombu," a Bantu word for the vegetable okra.

English is filled with words that originally came from other languages. Can you think of any?

IS THERE AN OFFICIAL AMERICAN RELIGION?

Nope. There isn't any one religion that Americans have to join and there isn't an official church, synagogue, mosque, or temple that Americans must attend. In fact, religious freedom—the freedom to choose how you want to pray, whether you want to pray, and what you want to believe—is one of the most important rules we live by.

We also have strict rules separating church and state. That means that the president isn't allowed to tell you what to believe, your mayor can't send you to church, and your public school principal isn't allowed to make you to take off your hijab, kipa, turban, cross, or other religious clothes or jewelry.

When winter's cold weather creeps in, the sky grows darker earlier. There are a bunch of holidays that brighten the neighborhood with twinkling lights and flickering candles. Can you name a few?

Why did our founders, more than 200 years ago, make religious freedom a rule? Well, because a lot of them came from countries where the king could tell you what to believe and punish you if you disagreed with him. Religious freedom has drawn immigrants to our shores for hundreds of years. Pilgrims and Puritans from England were some of the first people to come here for that reason. They endured voyages of two to three months or longer over the stormy, rough Atlantic Ocean in boats that were small and cramped—some were just the size of

a city bus! Many made the trip because they wanted to be free to go to their own churches, which were banned, or not allowed, in England.

William Penn was locked up in jail in England because he was a Quaker. He moved to America and started a new colony that welcomed people from all religions. His colony became one of our first states, and its name is based on his last name. Can you guess the state? If you guessed *Pennsylvania*, you guessed right!

HOW DOES AMERICAN MUSIC SOUND?

When you scan through different stations on the radio, what music comes on? You might hear thumping hip-hop beats, rousing orchestral marches, sentimental country love

songs, or screeching guitar solos. What you find is that there isn't one kind of American music, but a rich and varied songbook springing from all the different people here who have blended their musical traditions over time.

African Americans created the basis for blues, jazz, rock and roll, and hip-hop. In fact, today's rock music is the grandchild of the blues and jazz, two kinds of American music that started with songs sung by enslaved African Americans. Some of those songs were from the Western African nations where many of those men and women came from.

Hip-hop, a modern African American musical invention, often features rappers and DJs scratching recorded albums. Even though it's a totally original art form, where would hip-hop be without the first gramophone records that the German immigrant Emile Berliner invented 100 years earlier?

Meanwhile, some of the most popular American tunes were written by immigrants who expressed their deep connection to America through music. Songwriter Irving Berlin wrote the famous American songs "God Bless America" and "White Christmas," but he was originally from Russia and named Israel Beilin. His family moved to America to escape the violence and threats they faced in Russia simply because they were Jewish.

Music touches people even if they don't understand the lyrics. American music is popular all over the world in part because of the layered sounds unique to American culture.

WHERE DO AMERICANS LIVE?

It probably won't surprise you to learn that most Americans are people who live in—you guessed it—America! But our country isn't the same from coast to coast or from top to bottom. Americans live and work near active volcanoes, the frozen Arctic, the hottest desert land on Earth, and everywhere in between!

America is home to some of the world's busiest cities—like New York, Chicago, Los Angeles, and Houston. And Americans invented modern-day suburbs, quieter neighborhoods just outside of big cities. We also cultivate some of the world's most fertile farms—our Midwest corn farms grow more plants than anyplace else on the planet. And our country is chock full of precious natural resources. There's even a state park in Arkansas where you can take home any diamonds you dig up!

Lots of Americans live in other countries too. Some go overseas for school, and some leave for work. Many Americans serve our country in the military—in branches like the Army and Navy—

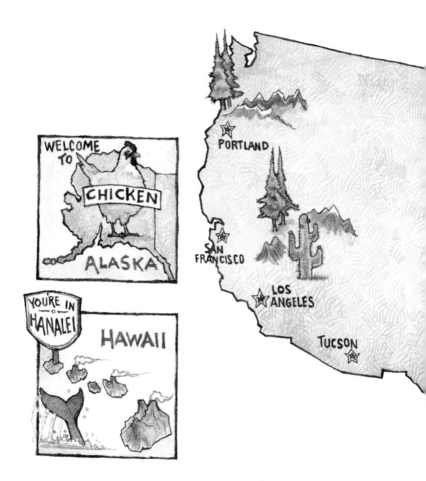

and live with their families all over the world on military bases. There are also lots of Americans abroad who volunteer to build schools or roads, or who heal the sick where doctors are scarce.

Some towns in America have very funny names. While Money, Mississippi; Chicken, Alaska; and Sandwich, Massachusetts, sound fun (and tasty!), what do you think happens in Lost City, West Virginia; Accident, Maryland; or Frankenstein, Missouri?

SO WHAT *DO* AMERICANS HAVE IN COMMON?

Have you noticed a pattern so far? We Americans are very different from one another. We come from different backgrounds, speak different languages, dance to different music, live in different climates, eat different foods, and practice different religions.

But we do have something very important in common: our Declaration of Independence, Constitution, and Bill of Rights. They are the documents that form the basis of our government, and they put into law a promise to respect our freedom, to allow us to live in peace by voting to elect our leaders, and to treat people equally. They make sure our government is "of the people, by the people, for the people."

These ideas unite us as Americans like no single food, song, or religion ever could. Why? Because America is a work in progress, always striving to be better, and these rules leave enough room for us to change and grow, together.

This means that even if we make bad laws, we can always fix our mistakes. That happened in 1882, when our country passed a cruel law discriminating against Chinese immigrants. Many Chinese people arrived at Angel Island off of San Francisco, where they were locked up and questioned for weeks, months, and even years. But because our government is set up to allow us to make laws better, we were able to change that law and others like it to be more welcoming of immigrants.

Did you know that democracy in America is actually older than the United States? The Haudenosaunee, also called the Iroquois, formed a confederacy of Native American tribes who tackled problems and made decisions peacefully as a group through talking and voting. Their example even inspired Benjamin Franklin, one of the founders of the United States.

One of the saddest parts of our history is that America had slavery. Bringing slaves into America was allowed for years after our Constitution was adopted. But there were people here who knew that slavery was wrong and struggled to end it. After the Civil War, Americans changed the Constitution to outlaw slavery by adopting the Thirteenth Amendment.

Are there laws or rules today that you believe should change?

HOW DO WE CHANGE OUR LAWS?

By voting! That's key to being an active citizen. When we vote, we elect leaders who make and change laws. If you were born here, you're an American citizen and can vote or even run for office when you turn eighteen. If you're an immigrant, you can become an American citizen, and after that you'll be able to vote or try to get elected yourself.

One very special job that's reserved for citizens who were born in America is probably the toughest job to get: President of the United States. But if you're an immigrant who has become a citizen, you can run for office in other elections in your neighborhood and your state. And anyone—young or old, American-born or immigrant—can help out on a campaign to elect the next mayor, senator, or school board member.

Back when homesteaders were moving to the Western frontier, some territories offered the right to vote to women and to noncitizens as a way to lure families to settle the wild and rough terrain.

It's exciting to volunteer on election campaigns, and kids can join the fun! You can talk to voters about what matters to you, make phone calls, knock on doors, color signs, and hand out leaflets to encourage your neighbors to come out and vote.

Did you know that babies born on airplanes flying over America are American citizens?

WHAT OTHER KINDS OF CHANGES HAVE AMERICANS MADE?

America is the land of opportunity, and we use our freedoms to change more than laws. Our inventions have transformed the way the world works, plays, sleeps, and eats. Americans designed the computers in your home and in your pocket, created the sport of basketball, invented the fast-food drive-through, made many important scientific breakthroughs, and were the first humans to fly to the moon!

Take the shots you get at the doctor's office; they hurt, but they save lives. The American-born son of Russian Jewish immigrants, Jonas Salk, invented the vaccine against polio, a disease that would paralyze or kill people who got it. He also shared his discovery with other scientists, doctors, and patients all over the world.

> Did you know that one of the world's longest bridges, San Francisco's Golden Gate Bridge, was designed to sway from side to side in its windy location? The bridge's inventive engineers were from all over: Cincinnati, Ohio; Latvia; and Switzerland. And the banker who helped pay to build it was an Italian immigrant who moved to San Francisco and who loved his adopted city.

American Elisha Otis invented the safe elevator that wouldn't come crashing down if the cables broke. Later, another American, Alexander Miles, created a new way for elevator doors to open and close that was safer for riders. Without these inventions and more, we'd never be able to have skyscrapers like we do today. Imagine climbing 102 stories to the top of the Empire State Building without an elevator!

And more immigrant inventors come to America than to any other country in the world. The inventor of the telephone, Alexander Graham Bell, was born in Scotland; the inventor of blue jeans, Levi Strauss, came from Bavaria; and even the inventor of American cheese, James L. Kraft, was originally from Canada!

WHAT ELSE
HAVE AMERICANS
INVENTED?

There are some American inventions that you use every day, like machines, tools, clothes, medicine, or food. Other kinds of progress may be harder to see and touch, even though they're very much a part of your life. Americans have used their ideas, their voices, and their hearts to make us stronger and healthier, and to break down the barriers that sometimes keep us apart.

American Dr. Charles Drew used his medical know-how to help a lot of people. He invented a way to preserve and ship blood to treat wounded soldiers during World War II.

His program collected enough blood to fill more than two Olympic-sized swimming pools. But he left his job when he was told to separate blood donated from African Americans and white Americans. He knew that was the wrong thing to do—as an African American, his blood would be separated from other donors' blood. We have since abolished that cruel and foolish rule.

Did you know that you had to take a test the minute you were born? Dr. Virginia Apgar, whose parents were from Poland, invented a way to check if newborn babies were healthy or if they needed extra medical care. More than 60 years after she invented it, hospitals still use the Apgar test to check a newborn's heartbeat, breathing, skin color, strength, and reflexes.

Cesar Chavez also broke down barriers. Even though he and his family worked very hard in the fields picking fruits and vegetables, they lived in run-down, unsafe neighborhoods with other farmworkers. Cesar wanted to help his fellow farmworkers, many of whom were Mexican Americans like him, so he and Dolores Huerta started a union

of farmworkers. They protested peacefully for better pay and safer places to work. After Chavez died, US President Bill Clinton awarded him the Medal of Freedom because he helped so many people.

Are there things you want to change in your school or neighborhood? How can you organize classmates and friends to make a difference?

SO, WHAT *IS* THE BIG DEAL ABOUT AMERICANS?

Looking close up at the American people, we see a lot of differences: so many languages and backgrounds, talents and interests, hopes and beliefs. It's almost like looking at a mosaic, where each individual tile has its own unique color and shape. But in our country, when one tile is laid next to millions of other unique tiles, it creates a colorful, vibrant picture.

The tiles never lose what makes each one special, but when you step back to take in the full image, you see a portrait of an America that is dynamic and lively. Our nation is powerful for the ways we work together, help one another, and learn from each other and from our history.

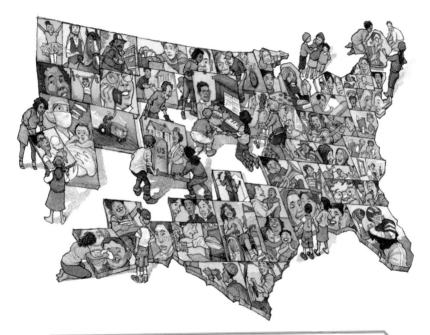

Ever wonder where your family is from? Ask your parents and grandparents for stories about when your ancestors came to America. No matter when it was or why they came here, you have a unique tile to add to America's mosaic. What will you do with it?

TIMELINE

Around 15,000–30,000 years ago The first Native Americans began settling the continent of North America. Over thousands of years, tribes spread over what is now known as the USA, all with different languages and cultures.

1000 Vikings from Northern Europe sailed to North America.

1492 Christopher Columbus and his crew made land in the Americas.

1570 The Iroquois Confederacy, the first democracy in what would later become the United States, was established.

1607 English colonists arrived in Jamestown, Virginia, the first lasting English colony in what would later become the USA.

1776 American colonies declared their independence from England, creating the United States of America.

1791 US Constitution with the Bill of Rights was ratified and became the supreme law of the land.

1808 Congress barred the importation of African slaves to America.

1840–1860 First of several waves of immigration to America from Europe. In this era, the majority of newcomers were from Ireland and Germany, and many practiced Catholicism.

1848   First workers from China arrived in San Francisco.

1848   Gold discovered in California, leading to a gold rush prompting thousands of people to move to California.

1865   Thirteenth Amendment to the Constitution ratified, abolishing slavery.

1869   Wyoming became first territory or state to grant women the right to vote.

1869   Transcontinental Railroad completed, opening up America's frontier to settlement.

1870   Fifteenth Amendment to the Constitution ratified, granting African American men the right to vote.

1870–1920   Second great wave of immigration to the US. In this period, 26 million people came to America— that means more people came to live here as immigrants during those years than had been living in America in 1850. Many of the new immigrants came from Eastern and Southern Europe as well as from the Americas and Asia.

1882   Chinese Exclusion Act barred immigrants to the US from China.

1885   Completed Statue of Liberty arrived in the US as a gift from France.

1886   America's first settlement house opened in New York City. It provided services and help to immigrants and poverty-stricken people.

1891 Law established a national office of immigration.

1892 Ellis Island in New York Harbor opened, welcoming more than 12 million immigrants over the next 62 years.

1898 Supreme Court ruled that children born in the US are citizens, no matter where their parents came from.

1910 Angel Island, off of San Francisco, opened as an immigration station on the West Coast.

1917 Congress passed a bill excluding all Asians from immigrating to the US and requiring all new immigrants to take a literacy test to get into the country.

1920 Women won the right to vote.

1924 Law passed that strictly limited immigration to the US based on the country where the immigrants were coming from (country of origin). This was the last of a series of such laws. After this point, immigration slowed down considerably for the next 40 years.

1924 Native Americans granted American citizenship.

1943 Chinese Exclusion Act repealed.

1965 President Lyndon Johnson signed the Immigration and Nationality Act of 1965, abolishing the country-of-origin quota system. Instead, the new law based immigration on keeping families together and inviting skilled workers to the US.

AUTHOR'S NOTE

America is exceptional in many ways, thanks in large part to its ever-refreshing population, which continually breathes new life into the old documents of its founding. You could tell the story of Americans from many different angles, because we all have our unique strengths and struggles. But what is undeniable is that so many of our achievements have been possible because democracy, freedom, and diversity commingle here to create an unusually dynamic, inventive society that has initiated progress in every realm. I hope this book inspires kids from all backgrounds to know what they, as Americans, are capable of achieving. That's why I offer glimpses of some of our great inventors—men and women who were imprinted with the advantages and challenges of their ancestries and driven by an abiding commitment to progress in this country. I also hope to show kids the strength in our diversity, a launchpad for opportunity, which is rendered all the more powerful and effective by the liberties at the heart of our democracy.

I consulted a lot of excellent resources as I researched this book, including US government websites such as archives.gov, nps.gov, and americaslibrary.gov; the websites of presidential libraries like the LBJ Library (lbjlibrary.org); and the websites of important foundations such as the Statue of Liberty–Ellis Island Foundation (libertyellisfoundation.org) and the Angel Island Conservancy (angelisland.org).

Some books that were particularly useful include:
- ★ *500 Nations,* by Alvin M. Josephy, Jr.
- ★ *America in 1492,* edited by Alvin M. Josephy, Jr.
- ★ *Coming to America,* by Roger Daniels
- ★ *US Immigration in the Twenty-First Century,* by Louis DeSipio and Rodolfo O. de la Garza
- ★ *America the Ingenious,* by Kevin Baker
- ★ *TIME-LIFE American Inventors: A History of Genius*
- ★ *A People's History of the United States,* by Howard Zinn
- ★ *The Story of American Freedom,* by Eric Foner

Don't miss the other fun and fact-filled books in this series!